Healing Pet Loss

Practical Steps for Coping & Comforting Messages from Animals and Spirit Guides

Marianne Soucy

ISBN-13: 978-1502334282

ISBN-10: 1502334283

Table of Contents

Praise for

Healing Pet Loss – Practical Steps for Coping & Comforting Messages from Animals and Spirit Guides

"Marianne's book came at the right time for me. I've been going through a really tough time with decisions around the health of my own 13 year old dog dealing with arthritis, pain and reduced quality of life. I started reading the book and within minutes, tears of gratitude filled my eyes. I immediately felt a sense of relief that I wasn't the only one feeling all these painful emotions. Marianne writes from her heart, and I felt 100% understood. Compassion and empathy comes from every page. Marianne's tells painful personal stories around her own precious animals, which makes her book real and relatable. She's been there.

What I particularly liked is that there is help and support in this book for a range of animal lovers. She provides practical techniques to cope with loss, stress, anxiety, and other painful emotions, in a gentle way, for those

- *preparing for the loss of an animal (if an animal is currently very ill or failing)*
- *already grieving the loss of an animal*
- *going through the unbearable pain of a missing animal*

The uplifting, loving words received through her own animals who had passed on, was a profound healing tool for me. The love, light and unconditional love every animal has for their human, is so apparent and came as waves of relief. She teaches gently the value of staying present, living here and now, finding ways to stay calm and that we grieve so deeply because we loved so deeply.

I can't recommend this book highly enough for anyone grieving the eminent or past loss of an animal. It gave me the tools I lacked to deal with my doggie's last days, to make it special and memorable for all involved - and to deal with the grief I know will follow. Thank you Marianne, this is an incredibly needed and valuable book. "

Liesel Teversham
Coach, Speaker, Author of "No Problem. The Upside of Saying No".

"I absolutely LOVE your book! This book is filled with helpful ways to heal. I am eternally grateful for this author. She has given me the tools to focus on the love more than the loss. I really loved all the action steps and the journal. Ways to celebrate the time with our loved ones is a wonderful idea and this book will help anyone who is healing through any loss. I highly recommend this book!!!"

Karen Palmer
Best-Selling Author of "Dogs are gifts from God" and "The Secret of Puppy Love".

"Marianne Soucy's book will bring hope and healing to many a pet lover. An animal companion showers unconditional love on you. The loss of that kind of precious love is heartbreaking. Marianne uses beautiful visuals, uplifting quotes and personal experiences that soften a broken heart. That animals continue to love and support and teach us from the other realm comes through so wonderfully through the stories the author shares from her own pet guides. If you're grieving the loss of a pet or anticipating death, don't think a moment. Buy a copy of this book and you'll return to it again and again for comfort and counsel."

Uma Girish
Author of "Understanding Death: 10 Ways to Inner Peace for the Grieving" and "Losing Amma, Finding Home: A Memoir of Love, Loss and Life Detours".

Preface

"When you are sorrowful look again in your heart, and you shall see that in truth you are weeping for that which has been your delight." ~ Khalil Gibran

You most likely found your way to this book because you have lost your beloved animal companion, and are finding it difficult to cope with the loss. Your pain is unbearable, and you may be finding that no one fully understands the depth of the love you shared with your trusted friend and the depth of the grief you are experiencing. When you lose your companion, you are losing a true and loyal friend, the one who was always there for you and comforted you when life was tough, whether it was a problem at work, with your finances, with your health or with relationships. Whatever the problem was, you always knew that your beloved animal companion would be there for you, listening, not judging, and loving you unconditionally. The one you could always count on to comfort you and help you cope with life's difficulties is the one who is now gone.

You had a very strong mutual bond with your pet, so losing your beloved companion hits you unbelievably hard. You may also be finding it difficult to concentrate on your work—even ordinary daily tasks may become difficult.

When your heart is broken after losing your companion, I know there is nothing I can say that can instantly make your pain go away, but I can guide you and help make your grief bearable, and I can help you learn to live with your loss.

I have also loved and lost animals that were close to my heart. Below you will find a description of the last day I shared with my beloved cat Pittiput.

Pittiput's Last Day: Losing a Beloved Animal Companion

"How lucky I am to have something that makes saying goodbye so hard." ~ A.A. Milne, Winnie the Pooh

I will never forget that day, standing with him in the vet's office.

"There is nothing more we can do for him," the vet said. "His body is shutting down, and it wouldn't be fair to him to let him suffer." It was as I had feared, but I still felt as if my world was falling to pieces and that part of me was dying right there. It was hard to comprehend that our precious orange cat, Pittiput, whom we had known and loved for ten years, would not be with us much longer. The vet wanted to euthanize Pittiput right away but fortunately, I had enough presence of mind to say that I wanted it to take place at home so Pittiput could be in his familiar surroundings and so I would have time to say goodbye. The vet was kind enough to accommodate me, and we arranged for him to come to our home a little less than five hours later.

I walked home from the vet, carrying Pittiput in his carrier. It was a half-hour walk, and I cried all the way. Fortunately, there was nobody around, so Pittiput and I could be in peace. I stopped to sit on a bench and connect with him, telling him what was going on and how much we loved him. It was a beautiful sunny morning in June, and I made sure Pittiput got one last chance to feel the sun and sniff the fresh air.

When I got home, I called my husband at work to tell him the bad news. He was devastated, and struggled through the rest of the day knowing that when he returned home our beloved Pittiput would be dead. Those hours spent waiting for the vet were very tough, but I was happy that I had insisted on home euthanasia, and that I had the time to say goodbye properly to Pittiput. I spent those hours doing everything I could to be present, to connect with him and express my gratitude and love for him. The vet arrived, and everything seemed to be over too quickly.

While I was waiting for my husband to come home and say his goodbyes to Pittiput, some of our other cats came by to sniff and look at him, and to say their own goodbyes.

We buried him and held a small memorial ceremony. We miss him deeply but keep the fond memories of him alive in our hearts.

~ Marianne Soucy

Introduction:
You are not alone in your grief

"If ever there is tomorrow when we're not together... there is something you must always remember. You are braver than you believe, stronger than you seem, and smarter than you think. But the most important thing is, even if we're apart... I'll always be with you." ~ A.A. Milne

When you are heartbroken after the loss of an animal companion, you may feel that you are alone in your grief, and that no one understands.

Many people do not recognize the loss of a pet as a valid reason to grieve and feel deep sorrow. You have probably heard statements like, "It was just a pet," or "you can just get a new one." Most people are not insensitive, but if they have not had a close bond with an animal, they may be unable to understand how much you are hurting after the loss. Moreover, the depth of your pain makes them uncomfortable.

I am here to let you know that you are not alone in your grief, and that you have come to the right place.

As I just described above in the story of Pittiput's last day, I have been there too, and I will be there again. I have several times lost an animal companion that I loved more than I thought possible. One was cruelly taken from me when I was a child, without me having a chance to say goodbye; another was killed tragically by a car. Most recently, I lost my "soul sister", my constant companion through twelve years, Kia, when she died all alone in an animal hospital without me by her side.

In this book, I will share insights and action steps that will help you cope with the death of a beloved animal companion. A loss so significant is not something you just "get over," but I am here to give you hope that your grief will be bearable, and that you will be able to live with your loss while keeping the love alive in your heart.

Chapter 1:
When Your Pet Is Dying

"And can it be that in a world so full and busy, the loss of one creature makes a void so wide and deep that nothing but the width and depth of eternity can fill it up."

~ Charles Dickens

Realizing your beloved pet is dying is heartbreaking, and can be difficult to deal with. In this chapter, I will provide you with useful information and suggestions, as well as action steps that you can take right away to prepare for a peaceful and dignified farewell for your pet.

Pets as members of the family

The bond we develop with our pets is very strong and can sometimes go even deeper than that which we have with our human family. This connection goes beyond words, beyond thoughts, beyond judgment and beyond conditions. We connect with our pet especially from the heart. Consider the bond you have with your pet—I bet you have no doubt it is a heart-to-heart or soul-to-soul connection.

This is why the grief you experience following the death of your pet is so deep, and why the grief is already deep as the death of your pet is approaching. The deeper the love, the deeper the grief—those two go hand in hand.

Emotions and physical reactions

When your beloved animal companion is dying, you are likely to experience a wide range of emotions:

- sadness
- depression
- irritability
- anger
- restlessness
- tiredness
- inability to concentrate
- constant worry
- desperation
- debilitating fear of losing your companion

You might also experience physical reactions such as nausea or feeling as if you have a knot or pain in your stomach, or other symptoms such as sleeplessness, loss of appetite, depression and so on.

When you think about losing your beloved pet, it feels like someone is ripping your heart out; you feel like you are falling apart. I know all these feelings; I experienced them when I knew my orange cat, Pittiput, was dying, and again when it became clear my precious cat Kia was not going to live much longer.

Grieving when your pet is dying

When your pet's health deteriorates and you know his or her life with you is ending, you are likely to feel a strong desire to help them get better, or at least not suffer, and possibly helplessness, regret or even anger because you are unable to do more.

Allow yourself to feel the way you do, and learn to stay with and accept the feelings of grief and loss that overwhelm you—the situation is as it is. If there is nothing you can do to improve the situation, strive to be present in the midst of it all. Make the decision to be there for your pet.

Practice being with your pet consciously and really try to appreciate the time you have left together, rather than dwell on loss and pain. It is easier said than done, but try to let go and not resist. If you can do this, it will help make your remaining time together more peaceful.

Action steps

1) Daily meditation

Take steps to become calm, centered and in balance. This will enable you to be there fully for your animal companion during the last part of their life with you. When you are calm, you will be better able to take actions and make choices you can live with after your pet is gone, and better able to spend quality time with your beloved pet while you still can. Taking steps to becoming centered during this challenging time will help you avoid making decisions out of fear and emotional distress that you might regret after your pet has died. When you are more at peace, you will be better able to ensure that your animal companion dies in peace and with dignity.

To help you be fully in the moment with a clear mind no matter what happens, meditation can be very helpful. If you are not doing some kind of meditation or deep relaxation on a daily basis, now is a good time to start—you will be doing both your pet and yourself a favor. (See also, Chapter 9, Taking care of yourself after the loss of a pet.)

2) Start doing some research

a) Find a vet in your area you feel comfortable with who can provide the care your pet needs. If you are considering home euthanasia, make sure your vet provides that service. (Do not try to do it yourself! If your pet needs to be euthanized, a vet must do it.)

b) Have you looked for alternative or supplementary treatments? Even if your pet cannot be cured, there may be ways to make your pet's last days or weeks more comfortable. Reiki, shamanic journeying and flower essences are just a few.

c) If your pet requires special care, think about whether you will be able to provide it at home. Working together with a vet who provides home hospice care may be an option for you.

3) Determine your pet's quality of life

Here are some basic questions to ask yourself when you are trying to determine your pet's quality of life:

- Is your pet eating and drinking?
- Does your pet still have the will to live?
- Is your pet withdrawing from the rest of the family?
- Is your pet still happy to see you?
- How does your pet react to touch?
- Is your pet still responding to treatment, or is it time to stop trying to cure him? Collaborate with your vet on this one.

A tool that many find helpful is a Quality of Life Assessment. You can do an Internet search for "pet quality of life assessment" to find out if you can benefit from it.

In addition to the visible signs you are looking for when trying to answer the questions above, you can also connect directly with your pet and ask your questions through meditation, animal (telepathic) communication, shamanic journeying, journaling, etc. Ask your pet to give you an unmistakable sign when he or she is ready. (This sign is not something you determine beforehand, but something you will recognize when it happens.) The answer may also be revealed to you through distinct synchronicities. (Read more about synchronicities in Chapter 7.) When you do receive an indication or sign, you will know it. There might be a single powerful sign or a sequence of smaller signs. Send your intention out to your pet and out into the universe.

Euthanasia versus letting nature take its course

As pet owners or animal guardians we want to make sure that our beloved animal companions do not suffer, and we want to do the best we possibly can to give them a peaceful death, preferably at home with us. As our pet's caretakers, we are the ones who have to make the heartbreaking decision of whether or not to euthanize when our beloved pet gets ill and death approaches.

But how can we be sure that euthanizing our pet is the right thing to do, and how do we make sure we do not euthanize prematurely—or prolong our pet's suffering unnecessarily? Making the wrong decision about euthanasia can leave you tormented by feelings of guilt and regret. The feeling of letting your beloved pet down is unbearable.

The decision to euthanize a beloved pet is often extremely difficult to make. If you don't know what is wrong with your pet and you don't know if your pet can be cured, it can be hard to determine how long to look for diagnoses and cures, and when to let go. You may even have to make this decision without knowing what is wrong with your pet.

It can be helpful to keep in mind that although we might prefer that our pet die a "natural" death, the life our pets have with us does not follow the normal "course of nature". Our pets are domesticated animals: they are cared for and fed by us, and probably spend much of their time indoors. This is not the life they would have if they lived naturally as wild creatures.

Whether and when to euthanize your pet depends on your considered evaluation. Each case is different. Use all the research you have done to determine to the best of your ability what your pet's quality of life is, and what is best for your pet.

If you follow the steps outlined above, you will have a good chance of providing your pet with a peaceful and graceful death, and to avoid being overwhelmed by feelings of guilt and regret after your pet's death. Instead, you will achieve peace of mind, knowing you did the very best you could for your beloved. After all those years of loving you unconditionally, your pet deserves that you do your best.

With life and death, there are so many unknowns, and we can never know for sure what will happen next. Life often has plans of its own, so things might not always happen as you would prefer. Nevertheless, doing your best is what counts—intentions do matter.

Giving your pet permission to die

When your pet is dying and you are facing the imminent loss of your beloved animal companion, it can be difficult to come to terms with the situation and deal with it.

There are many situations where you might think, it is not fair or it cannot be happening. For instance, if your pet is still young but was either badly injured or has become very sick, and will pass on much sooner than you had expected. Another example would be if your pet is getting old but has a severe illness that is causing him or her great pain or discomfort. In either of these situations, you can easily end up in denial and resistance because life does not seem to be fair. (See also Chapter 4, When life feels unfair)

Fear of separation

If you are like me, the bond you have with your pet is very loving and very strong. Therefore, when you can see that the death of your pet is approaching, the fear of losing your close and constant companion may cause you to slip into denial; the thought of being without someone you love so much can be too painful to acknowledge.

Denial

Failing to accept the approaching death of your pet will cause more pain and prolong the suffering, not only for you but also for your pet. Your pet might respond to your holding on to them by hanging on to life longer than they should.

A compassionate gift

This is the time when you have an opportunity to give your pet one of the most compassionate gifts we can give: permission to die. This simply refers to letting go and allowing your pet to move on.

Letting go can be followed not only by deep sadness, but also by deep peace because the struggle within you has calmed down. You have accepted that your animal companion's time with you in their physical form will soon end, and their soul is now free to continue its journey.

It is important to note that giving your pet permission to die does not necessarily mean that your companion will die right away (although that sometimes happens, especially if one or both of you have been hanging on). Neither does it mean that you have decided whether your pet will die a natural death or by euthanasia. The acceptance and letting go is internal and enables you both to achieve inner peace that will make your pet's death more peaceful and graceful. It will give you the clarity and focus to be there for your pet and to make the decisions that are best for them.

Saying goodbye

Make sure to make time to say goodbye to your beloved animal companion. You do not have to wait to the last minute; choose a time that feels right for you and your companion when you have peace around you. Sit quietly together; experiencing the closeness, the bond and the love you share. Feelings of sadness and fear will come too; just let the feelings happen and keep returning to the experience of being together. Imagine you are both enveloped in peace and light, perhaps calling on your spirit guides to come and assist you.

When it feels right, express your gratitude and love to your companion, speaking from the heart. Let your companion know how much he means to you, and that you are going to miss him very much, but that you also understand that it will soon be time to leave. Give your pet permission to die when it is right for him, and say your goodbyes.

As you say your goodbyes, know deep in your heart that the love you share will never die. Know that you will always be able to access that deep love for your animal companion in your heart.

"To live in hearts we leave behind is not to die." ~Thomas Campbell

Create your final happy memories together

It is a heartbreaking and very difficult situation to be in when your beloved animal companion is dying and you know you have a very short time left together. However, you can use this situation to create something beautiful, an opportunity you do not have if your beloved animal companion dies suddenly. The fact that you have time together with your pet, even if only a short time, is in a sense a blessing, because you have a final chance to do something to make your animal companion happy. You can:

- Be there with and for your pet.
- Make your pet's last days easier and filled with love.
- Ease the transition—even by simply being there.
- Say goodbye and express your gratitude to your pet.

Give your pet a perfect day.

Giving your pet a perfect day is a wonderful idea. You can read about it in "The Perfect Day," by Jon Katz in Slate magazine. This article gives a beautiful example of how you could give your pet a perfect day and create some beautiful and lasting memories.

Here are some suggestions for your inspiration:

Make a list of all the things your pet loves to eat, the things they love to do, and the places they love to go. Then create a perfect day for your pet filled with as many of your pet's favorite foods, things, etc., as possible, remembering to take into consideration what your pet is in shape to handle and what type of pet you have. Your pet's perfect day might not consist of many activities or of going places; it could simply be getting a special treat and spending quality time with you while you express your love and gratitude—being present with them without distractions.

My last weeks with Kia

When my cat Kia was dying, I didn't just create one perfect day; I made her final weeks extra special, giving her as much attention—and space—as she needed. One of the things she loved was lying in the open doorway facing the garden, sniffing the fresh air and looking at the birds outside. I would be in the kitchen next to her, baking a pie or doing other kitchen work, while keeping an eye on her—and she keeping an eye on me. There was a special closeness and understanding between us during those moments. At night, she loved to sleep right next to my pillow, so her head was close to mine. During her last weeks, she also developed a habit where she would lie on a giant teddy bear we have sitting on the floor. As she was lying on that bear, she would knead and look up at us for extended periods with deep, gentle love. I always felt she could see right into my soul and during those last weeks her "soul gazing" intensified.

What could you do to either create a perfect day for your pet or make your pet's last days extra special?

A message from an animal companion

A week before she died, my beloved Kia gave me these words of advice and comfort. May they bring comfort to you in your time of grief and loss.

My body is tired, but my spirit is free. My spirit can never be in pain when I am surrounded by so much love. You can best help me by holding a sacred healing space of love and light for me to rest in.

My spirit is well and always will be, knowing that nothing can separate our souls anymore. In your journeys and dreams, I will be there to comfort and guide you, as you will comfort and guide me.

It was a blessed day when we met, and I will be forever grateful.

Chapter 2:
Allowing Yourself to Grieve

"There is a sacredness in tears. They are not a mark of weakness, but of power. They speak more eloquently than ten thousand tongues. They are the messengers of overwhelming grief, of deep contrition and of unspeakable love." ~ Washington Irving

It is natural to grieve the loss of your animal companion, although your reaction might not be what you expected. Your loss might have hit you harder than you thought it would, and you might be unable to stop crying. You might even feel that you are grieving more for the loss of your pet than you did when a human friend or family member died. On the other hand, your reaction might be shock and numbness, and you might find that you cannot cry at all.

Whatever you are feeling, it is okay—there is no right or wrong way to grieve. If the feelings of pain and sorrow are unbearable, you might find some comfort in reflecting on the following:

You are only grieving so deeply now because you loved so deeply.

The first step is to allow yourself to grieve, to allow the feelings of grief and sorrow to be there, and to allow yourself to experience what you are feeling without judgment. What happens if you try to stop looking at grief and love as separate? Can you let the love and the grief touch you without labeling or resisting?

A lot of the pain of grief comes from our resistance to accepting what has happened, and resistance to feeling pain. In fact, at first there is often an overwhelming feeling of "This can't be happening."

Try to take a little time—maybe while listening to relaxing music or a guided meditation—to watch and experience the feelings you are having. Through allowing rather than resisting the grief, it will be easier for you to avoid getting stuck in suffering. This will be painful at first, but it will make your grief more bearable and manageable.

Grief and love are not really separate, just as you and your pet are not really separate. The deep bond you have with your pet is not limited to the body or the physical—this connection and bond of love goes beyond death, beyond the physical realm. The love you shared is real and is still alive in both you and your pet.

The grieving process

Grieving is a process we all go through when we lose someone we love, and how we experience and handle grief is very individual. Grieving does not happen according to a schedule, but often comes in waves with various emotional and physical symptoms, some more dominant than others. Below is a list of symptoms you might experience or recognize from your own grieving:

- sorrow or overwhelming sadness
- yearning
- emptiness
- loneliness
- guilt
- anger
- helplessness
- insomnia

- difficulty concentrating

In addition to the symptoms above, some people may dream of their deceased pets or even see or hear them.

Nowadays most people's lives are so busy that there is hardly any time to grieve. We are expected to function more or less normally immediately after our loss or shortly thereafter. We might suppress the feelings of grief because they are too painful and difficult to handle. Denying our grief or suppressing our feelings is healthy for us neither now nor in the long term.

Exercise: Write two letters

The exercise I will share with you here can be a powerful healer. It involves writing a letter to your companion and receiving one back from them. It allows you to reconnect with your deceased companion, and helps you deal with the emotions surrounding the loss. The exercise is in two parts:

1.

In the first part of the exercise, you write a letter to your animal companion. Find a quiet place and choose a time when you will not be disturbed—you could perhaps listen to some soothing music or do a little meditation first. Then sit down with pen and paper (it works best when writing by hand) and write the letter. Write down everything you need to say to your beloved companion in this letter—how is your life without them? What are your feelings, thoughts and concerns?

2.

In the second part of the exercise, you write a letter from your companion to you. Imagine being your pet, and allow yourself to become calm as you start writing their message to you. Don't think too much while doing this; just let the writing flow as you imagine being your loved one writing a letter back to you.

Make sure you do both parts of this important exercise.

Chapter 3:
How To Deal With Guilt after Pet Loss

"To forgive is to set a prisoner free and discover that the prisoner was you." ~ L.B. Smedes

The loss of a beloved animal companion is often accompanied by intense feelings of guilt and regret. You will probably find yourself regretting things you did or failed to do before, during, or after your beloved companion's death. You might also experience a need for forgiveness, yet at the same time believe that you cannot or should not be forgiven.

Perhaps you decided to euthanize your animal companion because they were in pain, and now you are not sure you did the right thing.

It could be that you did not have the money to pay for expensive treatments when your animal companion was very ill, and are now feeling overwhelmed with guilt and regret.

You may regret not having enough time (or taking the time) to spend with your companion.

You may feel that you are at fault for not providing a better quality of life for your animal companion.

You may blame yourself for ignoring or missing warning signals or other signs.

The feelings of guilt and regret can be hard to deal with and let go of. You can get far by learning to accept the feelings—for example, through meditation—but the mind will often torment you with thoughts like:

- Did I do the right thing?
- Why did I not handle it better?
- If I had been there, I could have prevented my pet's death.
- If only I had spent more time with him (or her).

If you look at whatever feelings of guilt and regret you have in connection with the death of your beloved animal companion, you will notice that many are irrational. Most likely, you did the best you could and probably could not have done anything differently.

If you could communicate directly with your companion right now, what do you think they would say to you? And even if you could have done things differently, do you think your companion would have had a different message for you? Would your companion not show you compassion and forgiveness in either case?

Guilt, self-blame and forgiveness

There are many reasons why we might feel guilty after the death of a pet. We love our animal companions so much and feel a huge sense of responsibility, and we want to give our companion the best care possible. When our beloved companion dies, we can easily end up judging and blaming ourselves, consumed by guilt, and finding it very difficult or even impossible to forgive ourselves.

If you find yourself deep in remorse and guilt, and are unable to forgive yourself when your animal companion dies, the grieving process can become exceedingly difficult and long lasting. Guilt, blame and being unable to forgive—either someone else or yourself—is holding on to something or wanting something to be different than it is. It is not accepting the present moment or what led to the present moment. But because you want to change something that cannot be changed, blame or guilt is futile.

The first step toward recovery is to enter a state of inner peace—for instance, through meditation—and from there look at the situation and the events leading up to your pet's death. Look at it without judging, and accept responsibility for your part in what happened.

Questions to ask yourself

1. Do you feel responsible for your pet's suffering or death?
2. Could you have done something differently?
3. What have you learned from this situation?
4. What will you do differently if you find yourself in a similar situation?
5. What can you do now?

Feeling guilty and blaming yourself or someone else, keeps you in the pain. It prevents you from taking a step into the unknown future you are facing. In the case of pet loss, there is an underlying denial, a refusal to accept the loss, or a refusal to accept the way it happened. This separation feels like a part of yourself has been split off or taken from you.

When you used to think of yourself and your life, your pet was always part of it—part of you and part of your life. Without your pet, there is a huge emptiness. Allow yourself to feel that emptiness. Through surrendering to reality, you will reach an inner peace that will follow you wherever you go, and realize that the love you shared with your pet has not been lost and will always be a part of you.

Mindfulness exercise

Acknowledging and accepting that things happened as they did, and that you acted the way you did, is not an easy thing to do. It does not mean that you have to approve of it—there is no judgment involved. It simply means that you are facing the facts about what happened and what you did. Just mentally telling yourself to accept it, is not enough, especially if it involves the suffering or death of your animal companion. Taking time to acknowledge the grief and allowing the grief and guilt to be there is an important step on the way in healing from pet loss.

Can you allow the feelings of grief to be there without judging or blaming yourself? Take a little time every day to practice just being with whatever feelings you have. Be mindful and aware of what is going on inside you—your feelings and thoughts. Practice just monitoring what you are feeling and thinking, but without judging.

Feelings of resistance may surface. When they do, allow them to be there and notice the peace and stillness that is underlying all your thoughts and feelings, even those that are irrational or chaotic. Observe what happens within you. Who is the observer? You are not your thoughts or feelings—they change constantly.

Do a daily meditation or deep relaxation where you practice observing and not judging or blaming, and see what happens.

Action steps—a summary

1. First, meditate to calm your mind, emotions and body (for example, listen to some soothing music or do a guided meditation such as the Inner Peace Meditation (see resources section at the back of the book).
2. Allow yourself to experience the situation you are in, the grief and the loss, and notice what thoughts and emotions come up. Do this without labelling or judging!
3. End by asking yourself the five questions above. Write down the answers (in longhand) in a journal or notebook.

Besides setting aside time for these action steps, during your daily activities you can also practice being mindful and notice when you go into "self-blame" mode. When you do, try not to identify with the thoughts and feelings; instead, practice just watching. Return to these action steps whenever you need to.

Kia's death—my own experience with guilt after losing a beloved animal companion

One of the toughest emotions to deal with after pet loss is guilt. The guilt after the death of a beloved pet can be so devastating that you have no idea how you can go on. This happens especially if your pet's death did not occur in the peaceful way you had planned or hoped for. That is exactly what happened when I lost my beloved cat Kia in 2012.

She did not die peacefully at home with my husband and me — no, she died in the animal hospital, less than 24 hours after she was admitted, despite the fact that three different vets had examined her and said that she was at no immediate risk.

Imagine the unbearable guilt that washed over us when we got a call at 5 a.m. telling us that Kia had passed away during the night. The feeling of having let her down was stronger than almost anything I have ever experienced, because she meant so much to me and deserved a peaceful death at home with us.

Whenever a beloved animal companion dies, you will experience grief, as each animal companion and the connection you have with them is unique. So, even though I had lost animal companions before and dealt with the grief in each case, the grief and guilt still came after the loss of Kia. Because of the way her death occurred, the guilt was extra strong this time. My husband and I talked through everything that had happened many times and agreed that we had done our best, and that if we found ourselves in the same situation, would most likely do the same again.

How to let go of guilt—words of wisdom from an angel cat

One day, as I was struggling with guilt after losing my beloved Kia, I decided to connect with her to ask her for insights into how to deal with these feelings. The following is what happened.

As I connect with Kia, I find myself standing on a beach in the early morning. I hear the waves gently lapping on the shore, the air is fresh and it is only just beginning to get light. I can still see some stars, especially one star in front of me a little above the water on the horizon, which is bigger and clearer than the rest. It blinks a couple of times and "flashes out" toward me. Instantly, Kia is sitting next to me.

I greet her warmly, and she looks at me with gentle, loving eyes. She says calmly, "Always return to the present. It is not in the past but in the present moment, you will connect with me. That is the place to connect and rest without blame and judgment. That is the place to experience the love we shared and always will share. And it is in the present moment you can access the fond memories without regret but instead with joy.

"Memories are good, but when you go straight to the memories without anchoring in the present moment, you avoid and resist the present, and live in pain, guilt and regret.

"It is when you fully realize that you can access me and my love right here in the present that all guilt and regret will fall away, and you will not only remember our time together with love and joy but also experience my presence in the now, for I am with you wherever you go.

"Since we are one, we can still be together though we take different paths. There is no separation, and we will be together again.

"You experienced guilt so you could learn forgiveness, for when you walk the path of compassion, forgiveness is the key. And forgiveness includes others as well as yourself. Only when you can truly forgive can you embrace compassion. Surrendering to the present moment is the key to both.

"Just keep returning to the now and you will find me there."

I give thanks to Kia for her wise words and say goodbye. It is my wish that her deep insight and words of wisdom will bring you comfort and inspiration in dealing with your own grief after the loss of your animal companion.

Exercise for reconciliation and forgiveness

The ancient Hawaiian practice of reconciliation and forgiveness, Ho'oponopono, is something I have found to be helpful when struggling with guilt after the loss of an animal companion.

I will not go into the theory and background here, but simply introduce you to this practice and invite you to try it out. Modern practice of Ho'oponopono is actually quite simple: You set some time aside when you can be uninterrupted and repeat the following mantra. The order of the statements may vary slightly depending on where you read about it. You can reverse statements 3 and 4 if you like. This is the order that I generally prefer.

1) I am sorry. 2) Please, forgive me. 3) I love you. 4) Thank you.

Say all of the above statements one after the other, and repeat over and over (either within yourself or aloud). While you are doing this, allow yourself to feel whatever emotions come up, and look at the thoughts without judging—just observe.

I find it also works well when I do it "in the background," so to speak, while doing yoga, taking a shower, or going for a walk, just to cite a few examples. Doing it in the background can make it easier to free the mind from trying to control or thinking too much. You could also try this technique with some relaxing music.

When you use the practice in connection with pet loss, your thoughts will at first circle around your animal companion, the pain of the loss, and your feelings of guilt, regret, and self-blame. After a while, you might find something interesting happening: memories of people, places and events from other times and situations in your life may enter your mind. They might seem to have nothing to do with your current loss, but these past events or situations are most likely unresolved and coming up now so that you can deal with them and release them. One of the benefits I have experienced when using this practice after pet loss is that it not only allows you to deal with feelings of guilt but also eases you into an experience of love and gratitude. It helps you change your perspective from one of focusing on the pain of the loss and feelings of guilt, to one of love and gratitude.

Try it out for yourself.

I'll see you in the stars

"Perhaps they are not stars in the sky, but rather openings where our loved ones shine down to let us know they are happy." ~ Inuit saying

After the death of your pet, you might feel as if all the light has gone from your life and you are surrounded by darkness. But death is like the night that follows the day:

If you allow yourself to be in and experience the darkness, you will see—like the night sky—that the darkness is full of stars.

I received this image when I was outside in my garden one night watching over one of my cats, who was sniffing around in the bushes: one of the stars came down and turned into my deceased cat, Pittiput. We sat together for a while, just being with each other in peace, looking at the night sky. Then he went up into the sky again, turning into a twinkling star. Simple but beautiful imagery.

If you feel as if there is only darkness after your beloved pet has died, try to go outside one night when it is clear, and look at the stars. Send a blessing to your deceased pet as you watch the stars.

Lessons learned—let your animal companion be your teacher

We all make mistakes, but some mistakes can be harder to forgive and let go of than others. Two things you can do that will help you not only to move forward with your life but also to honor your beloved pet is to honestly look at all the things you could have done differently, and then decide to learn from those "mistakes" and handle things differently next time.

As I mentioned before, you most likely did the best you were capable of at the time. Faced with a similar situation now, you might think and act differently, but that does not mean you should blame yourself for what happened before.

Instead, let go of judgment and blame, and instead let your animal companion be your teacher. Honor your companion by learning from the life, the love and the challenges you experienced together.

Your animal companion would want you to have a good life. Think back, wasn't your companion communicating this to you when they were alive? Your companion was there for you and would not want you to suffer now.

Selected messages from an animal companion in the afterlife

Animals are wonderful teachers. My beloved cat Kia has communicated many wise and comforting messages to me. I will share a few of them in the hope that her loving and wise words might bring you comfort and peace in your grief.

"My love for you is unconditional and eternal. I loved you through your challenging times, and this last event is no different. How could I stop loving you? I could not stop loving you, just as you could not stop loving me. It is just not possible. A love unconditional is exactly that: without conditions."

"What you need now is to extend that unconditional love to yourselves. You know deep in your heart that you did the best you could and with the best of intentions."

"What happened to being in the present moment? You fear that, because you think it involves letting go and losing me. If you allow yourself to be in the present and let go of me, you will see that I am not gone and that you can never lose me. Think of when you were out at work and I was home. You felt and trusted the connection with me, even though you could not see me. Reconnect with that same trust now—I'm right behind the veil, one breath away."

"When you rest in presence, everything happens as it is supposed to. There is no right or wrong. Practice being in the field beyond right and wrong. When you manage that, you will truly see me."

~ Kia

Chapter 4:
When Life Feels Unfair: Insights from an Angel Cat on Pet Loss

"When you lose someone you love, you gain an angel you know." ~ Author unknown

Losing a beloved animal companion is a heartbreaking experience, but if you lose your animal friend in a way that leaves you wondering why it happened and how life could be so unfair, then the pain of the loss can be even greater.

One such example can be a puppy that dies tragically and suddenly. This happened to a woman who contacted me some time ago. It can be hard to see any sense, fairness or meaning in that. You may wonder why innocent, pure souls die prematurely, suddenly or even violently.

I decided to ask my angel cat Kia for her insights and advice. As I mentioned in a previous chapter, my beloved cat Kia died suddenly and all alone in an animal hospital. The only thing that brought my family and me real comfort and helped us cope was when I decided to contact Kia and communicate with her directly. Her words of wisdom were truly healing, and she has been a great source of wisdom and healing for many others and myself ever since then. I asked her how people could cope when something so tragic and unfair takes place as the sudden death of a four-month-old puppy. This is what happened:

I prepare for my connection with Kia by becoming present in my body, filling it out with my awareness. I take a deep breath and relax as I exhale. I focus on my feet, allowing them to send out their roots deep into the earth below—the firmness, grounding, nurturing, stability and support. When I am firmly grounded, I focus on the upper part of my body, allowing it to grow taller and taller, reaching high up in the sky. Water and land are below me. The sun is rising, and the beauty and stillness give me a feeling of deep peace. As I reach the peace, I hear Kia's voice:

"It is not about how you die, it is about how you live," she says. "Of course, it is important and admirable to strive for a conscious, peaceful death and to prepare so you will face death without fear, but we normally don't know when it is our time to go, so your task is to live fully, allow yourself to love and be loved and let go of fear and whatever else is preventing you from becoming who you truly are.

You humans can learn much from animals: Watch how we live fully in the present moment, how our joy is unrestricted and how we are able to love unconditionally. A young animal that has lived fully but dies, perhaps before it is one year old, has lived more fully, openly and completely than many humans [in their entire lifetime].

As we are all each other's teachers, let your focus be not on the why, on how unfair it is or on how painful, but on the celebration of the life that was. Celebrate that life and embrace what it was here to teach you.

What were some of the unique qualities it had that you can implement in your own life and thereby not only honor the one you lost but also grow and evolve as a human being?"

"Thanks, Kia. Anything else?"

"No, that's it for now. Go practice being in the present moment, without fear or regrets—just being here now."

With that, the journey ends and I thank Kia again.

To me, her advice to celebrate the life that was—the beloved animal companion now deceased—and learn from him gave me wonderful insight, providing a perspective that brings hope, and even joy, to a situation that otherwise seemed hopeless.

How can you celebrate your animal friend, and what lessons were they here to teach you?

Chapter 5:
Journaling to Help You Deal with Pet Loss

"In your light I learn how to love. In your beauty, how to make poems. You dance inside my chest where no-one sees you, but sometimes I do, and that sight becomes this art."

~ Rumi

After the death of a beloved pet, one of the tools you can use to cope with the grieving process is journaling. Here are a few tips on how to get started.

- Write in longhand. Pen on paper is much more effective than typing, in my experience.
- Do not worry about correct spelling or grammar.
- Write what comes to mind; in other words, do "stream-of-consciousness writing."

A good time to journal is in the morning when you first wake up. Julia Cameron has written a useful book, The Artist's Way, in which she calls this practice writing "Morning Pages," and she says, "There is no wrong way to do Morning Pages.... They are about anything and everything that crosses your mind—and they are for your eyes only."

Writing Morning Pages might not seem like much, but I know from personal experience that it will have a distinct and positive effect on your life. So just keep doing them for a period, and you will see. The important thing about Morning Pages is to write them when you first wake up, before you are "completely" awake and before getting into your usual routines. One thing I particularly liked to do was to end with a positive affirmation. After all the stream-of-consciousness rambling, it gave me a positive focus to end with, and a good start to the day.

Other things to include in your journaling

Besides the stream-of-consciousness writing, you can also

- Write a letter, poem or tribute—if there is something you feel you need to say to your deceased pet, write it out in longhand (see also Chapter 2, Exercise: Write two letters).
- Draw or paint.
- Pay attention to your dreams, and write them down.

Questions for you to answer

Often, being more specific in your writing will help the healing process. For instance, you could answer the following questions:

- What are your favorite memories of your pet?
- What things did your pet like to do?
- In what ways did your pet improve your life?
- What unique qualities did your pet have?

Chapter 6:
How to Create Your Own Pet Memorial Ceremony

"When someone you love becomes a memory, the memory becomes a treasure." ~ Author unknown

A memorial ceremony is a good way to both honor and say goodbye to your beloved animal companion. A memorial ceremony does not need to be elaborate, and below are three simple but powerful steps you can take today. Here is what you can do.

1. Find a picture or photo of your deceased pet and put it where you can see it. If you feel inspired, you could make a photo collage. You might also use one of their favorite toys or some fur or feathers from your pet to help you feel the connection with them.
2. Light a candle and then just sit quietly with closed eyes for a while. You could have some quiet soothing music on in the background. Imagine yourself becoming centered and relaxed, then open your eyes and look at your pet's picture and the candle next to it.
3. Sit quietly for a while and imagine the connection between you and your pet; see it in your mind's eye.
4. Now it is time for you to express what you wish to communicate to your pet.
   - Read a favorite poem.
   - Read aloud a "letter" you have written to your pet.

     o   Share (aloud) fond memories of special moments you have of your pet.

Express gratitude to your pet and say goodbye. End the little ceremony in a way that feels right to you. Only your imagination puts limits on what you include in your memorial ceremony. Planting a tree, a bush or a flower is also a beautiful way to honor your animal companion's memory and legacy.

What can you include in your pet memorial ceremony that honors and expresses your love and connection with your trusted friend?

Chapter 7:
Synchronicities and Signs from the Pet in the Afterlife

"To live in hearts we leave behind is not to die." ~ Thomas Campbell

After the death of an animal companion, we often wish we could receive some kind of sign that our companion is okay in the afterlife. We want so much to reach out to our beloved companion and feel the connection once again, even if only for a brief moment—and we can.

If we can remain open and rise above heavy emotions, then synchronicities are bound to occur. The truth is that synchronicities will almost certainly occur, but if we are unable to recognize them, we will not know when we are missing them, will we? The key is not to go around looking for synchronicities; if you are open, and cultivate the attitude that anything is possible, synchronicities will find you!

Synchronicities

Synchronicities are common in healing, and I have experienced many synchronicities in connection with pet loss. Synchronicities are meaningful coincidences that show you there is a connection between and an overlapping of what is inside and what is outside—the inner and the outer. Synchronicities remind you that the universe is nurturing and supporting you. In connection with pet loss, synchronicities can be a bridge from the other side—a thinning of the veils between the worlds.

The following is a real-life synchronicity after the death of my beloved black-and-white Manx cat, Rumi.

Rumi and the cherry blossoms

Rumi died very suddenly and tragically; he was run over by a car while on one of his nightly rounds. Still in a state of shock a few days after the loss, my husband and I decided to break our routines and do something completely different. We went to a special theme/amusement park, somewhere we very rarely went, that is known for its garden-like (green) atmosphere.

It is a beautiful sunny spring day, still and calm. We are walking and talking about Rumi. We suddenly find ourselves standing in front of a group of magnificent cherry trees in full blossom with exquisitely beautiful pink flowers. Just as we become aware of the trees, they start releasing their flowers! There is a steady "snowfall" of pink flower petals. It is as if the cherry trees had purposely decided to release their flowers just at that moment. We look around and see no sign of a breeze or movement in the other trees; all is still and calm. Yet the cherry trees are shaking loose their blossoms, and this goes on for several minutes ... We are in no doubt that Rumi is reaching out to say farewell and let us know he is okay in the afterlife.

This was a magical experience that we will always remember.

Although synchronicities may not always occur, when they do, you feel that your prayer has been heard, and it becomes so much easier to have faith and to trust. Have you experienced a sign from your animal companion since he or she died that you know deep inside was a message for you?

Chapter 8:
A Gift of Peace from an Angel Cat

What we have once enjoyed we can never lose; All that we love deeply, becomes a part of us. ~ Helen Keller

Animals are wonderful teachers and have much wisdom to share with us in our daily life, and when we are struggling to cope with their loss.

The following is an account of a recent meeting I had with my precious cat Kia, who died in 2012 but continues to share her wisdom and love with me in meditations and shamanic journeys. I hope that this account will bring you peace and inspiration.

I am sitting on the train one morning; feeling drained by life and by stress and it is only 7 a.m.! I go within as much as I can, focusing on and imagining going into the heart center.

This time it seems to open up into a forest—like a Swedish forest. It is a beautiful sunny day, and there are trees and wilderness in all directions as far as the eye can see. There is peacefulness in the air, no feeling of hurry, and no sign of humans. There are trees all around, the majority of them are pine, but there are also birch and other trees.

I approach a lake. The large body of water draws me, and I look at the calm surface. I then see Kia sitting on a fallen tree beside the lake. She looks at me, and I am filled with a feeling of deep love, a yearning and a feeling of coming home.

I sit on the ground in front of the fallen tree and lean my back against it. Kia jumps down and settles beside me. I put my arm around her, feeling her familiar soft fur and warm body. I feel tears coming—I have missed her so much. For a moment I close my eyes and just sit there, letting the sun shine on me, warming and blessing me, feeling Kia against me, right where she is supposed to be.

"I have been missing you, too," she says. "You sometimes forget that in spirit we are one. Hold me in your thoughts and in your heart, and I am there."

"Are you okay, Kia?" I ask.

"I am fine. I am at peace, in perfect health, and living beyond time—being in the present. The more you are able to stay in the present, in a state of peace, the easier it is for us to keep the heart and spirit connection, and live with the constant realization that there is no separation. If you cannot get to peaceful, quiet places in nature, go within and find the peace there; and, as today, you will find that I will join you there."

She is quiet and looks at me—deep into my soul, with such love. She sees all of me and embraces me with her love. A deep feeling of peace and stillness emanates from her and holds us both in a timeless moment.

Then she blinks and in a moment, she is gone, and I am back on the train once again.

"Thank you, Kia. I love you so much. Thanks for your love, your wisdom and for being you."

Action step

Spend some time in nature and let the stillness and peace lead you to inner stillness and peace. If you do not have access to a peaceful spot in nature, you can use a meditation to reconnect with inner peace.

Chapter 9:
Taking Care of Yourself after the Loss of a Pet

"Just keep returning to the now - and you will find me there." ~ *Kia*

When you are grieving the loss of an animal companion, you may find yourself in alternating states of chaos, fear, anxiety, helplessness and sorrow. You may find it difficult to focus, and to sleep or rest.

During the daytime, you might be able to push your feelings down to a certain degree so you can do the things you need to do. However, when there are no more distractions or chores to be done, the feelings of loss, grief, sadness, guilt and emptiness come pouring in, along with memories of all the good times you had with your companion, and the realization that you will never experience those happy moments again. You have feelings of guilt and regret over things you wish you had done differently. So, you lie awake for hours, tossing and turning, and are even more exhausted the following morning.

Even under normal circumstances, you can feel how emotionally and physically weakened you are if you do not get proper sleep. So imagine what sleeplessness does to you when you are vulnerable after losing a companion.

Being in a state of grief affects all areas of your life: your mental state, your health, your relationships and your work—everything. Taking care of yourself and making sure you get proper sleep and rest is important after the death of an animal companion. It will help you to cope better with grief, and make it more bearable.

There are a number of other things you can do to take care of yourself during the period of grief:

- Take time to listen to calming, relaxing music, and play songs that remind you of your companion.
- Go for walks and spend time in nature.
- Eat healthy meals and be wary of emotional eating.
- Do a daily meditation or deep relaxation.
- Practices like yoga, tai chi, aikido, and similar practices work on your whole being, and are excellent ways of calming and strengthening the body and balancing the emotions while achieving clarity and focus.
- Practice gratitude. (I will go deeper into gratitude in the next chapter.)

Meditation

The practices of meditation and deep relaxation are known to relieve stress and provide relaxation. They are often used in the morning to help you relax, and become focused and present during your daily activities. But if you are having trouble sleeping after the loss of a pet, meditation or deep relaxation in the evening before bed can also help calm you enough to actually fall asleep and get some decent rest—that is my personal experience. The Inner Peace Meditation I have created is a very effective guided meditation with soothing nature sounds, and you can download it free from my website.

Chapter 10:
The Healing Power of Gratitude after Pet Loss

"Gratitude makes sense of our past, brings peace for today and creates a vision for tomorrow."
~ Melody Beattie

The loss of a pet often makes it almost impossible for us to see or feel anything but pain and sorrow. All the good times we spent with our pet, as well as the other blessings we have in our lives, seem to fade into the background as the overwhelming emotions of grief take control. While it is important to let yourself grieve, the feelings of sadness, emptiness, guilt and pain can sometimes be so strong that it is difficult to cope. The bond many of us have with our pet is very strong, and so is our grief.

Gratitude as a tool for healing

The value of gratitude has long been known, and studies have shown that gratitude—having a positive, appreciative attitude—contributes to better health, an elevated sense of well-being and faster recovery from illness.

While we may acknowledge gratitude's many benefits, it can still be difficult to sustain, especially in the midst of grieving the death of a beloved pet.

That is why practicing gratitude makes so much sense. When we practice giving thanks for the time with had with together with our pet, as well as for the blessings we have in our lives now, we give ourselves the chance to see all of life as a blessing, to see not just the grief and the pain, but also the love.

Remember that gratitude is not a blindly optimistic approach in which the bad or painful things in life are ignored or suppressed. It is more a matter of where we place our focus and attention. Pain and injustice exist in this world, but when we focus on the gifts of life, on all the fond moments with and memories of our pet, we gain a feeling of well-being. Gratitude balances us and gives us hope, allowing us to let go of the grief and really feel appreciative of having known such an amazing animal in our lives.

What is on your gratitude list? What things about your pet are you grateful for? What (or who) do you have in your life now that you are grateful for?

Some ways to practice gratitude

- Keep a gratitude journal in which you list things for which you are thankful. You can make daily, weekly or monthly lists. Keeping this journal where you can see it will remind you to think in a grateful way.
- Make a gratitude collage by drawing or pasting pictures.
- Practice gratitude around the dinner table, or make it part of your nighttime routine.
- Practice finding the hidden blessing in a challenging situation.
- When you feel like complaining, or things seem hopeless, make a gratitude list instead. You might be amazed by how much better you feel.
- Notice how gratitude is influencing your life and write about it, or express it in some way that feels right for you.
- A practice I like is to take a daily twenty- to thirty-minute walk with my husband. We practice being present during our walk, and we each share three things we are grateful for.

As you practice, an inner shift begins to occur, and you may be delighted to discover how content and hopeful you are feeling. That sense of fulfillment is gratitude at work, and little by little, it will be easier for you to move through pet-loss grief and achieve a state of inner peace and gratitude, feeling love rather than pain when you think of your beloved animal companion.

"Gratitude Journal"

Having a "Gratitude Journal" to fill out can be very helpful. See the resources section (www.HealingPetLoss.com/resources) for a link to my Gratitude Journal.

Chapter 11:
A Healing Meeting with an Animal Companion in the Afterlife

"Sometimes words are not necessary, and the most powerful healing and memorable moments often take place in silence. Stillness without and within brings peace and healing." ~ Kia

One very comforting way of gaining peace of mind is to contact your deceased pet in the afterlife through meditation, shamanic journeying or animal communication. I would like to share a healing meeting I had with my cat Kia about two weeks after she died, in the hope that it will bring you healing and inspiration. I first set the intention to meet Kia and find healing for us both, and I do my preparations for the meeting.

I find myself on a beach with my spirit helpers. Behind me are trees. Kia approaches from the right and sits down next to me.

"So we're on a beach today," says Kia, looking around and sniffing the sea air.

My spirit helper says, "You both needed healing, so I figured a trip to the beach would do you good."

We lie down in the sand, looking at the sky and listening to the waves. The sun is setting, and the sky turns red, orange, yellow and many more colors I cannot even describe. As the sun sets, a peace washes in over all of us as we rest. I doze off with Kia in my right arm, her head close to mine. She sighs, and I listen to her familiar breathing. She is where she belongs.

The next thing I know is waking up to the sound of waves and the fresh sea air on my face. It is morning now. I take a deep breath and feel refreshed. Kia is sitting next to me. She looks at me with infinite love in her eyes.

"Sometimes words are not necessary," says Kia, "and the most powerful healing and most memorable moments often take place in silence. Stillness without and within brings peace and healing. This time we have spent here in silence together will not only heal, but also stay with you forever, and bring you healing and peace when you bring up the image in your mind. Creating an image you can look at (by drawing it, for example) would also be helpful."

She gently rubs her face against me before leaving.

I thank her and my spirit helpers, and end the journey.

Action step

What can you create, such as a drawing, a poem, a piece of art or perhaps a song, which can be a physical representation of a fond memory, or a special feeling or experience you had with your pet?

Chapter 12:
How to Move Forward after the Death of a Pet

"If light is in your heart, you will find your way home." ~ Rumi

After the death of your pet, you will need to create new habits and routines for a life in which your pet is not with you in his or her physical form. When you have been grieving the loss of your pet for a while, you might reach the point where you feel the need to move on, but cannot seem to do it. You still feel overwhelmed by guilt, and stuck in the pain of the loss. One thing that might be blocking you is a feeling of guilt about "moving on," a feeling that you are somehow abandoning, forgetting or letting down your deceased pet.

So how do you move on with your life when your animal companion is gone? One thing I have noticed is that our mindset and even the words we use make a big difference. Let me give you an example. When you are thinking of creating a life after the loss of a pet, you are most likely using the phrase "move on" in your mind, just as I just did in the paragraph above:

- I want to move on, but do not know how.
- How do I move on after the death of my pet?
- I need to move on with my life, but how can I?

Let us look at what the phrase "move on" means to us. To me it implies some kind of separation, leaving something or someone behind. If you have lost a pet, it would seem to indicate leaving your pet—including the love and all the fond memories—behind. From this perspective, it is easy to see that "move on" is a term that might actually keep us stuck in grief.

People often say, "It is time to move on." What this usually means is that it is time to suppress and forget your feelings and memories. But see what happens when you change one little word. Instead of saying "move on," you can say, "move forward". "Moving forward" has an entirely different meaning and feeling to it, doesn't it? When I hear that phrase, I get a positive feeling, a feeling of carrying with me all the love, fond memories and lessons I learned from my pet. It is no longer suppressing and forgetting, but acknowledging and remembering. How do you feel the distinction between "move on" and "move forward"?

Remember the love

Suddenly it becomes easier to imagine a life after pet loss, because you realize that while your pet's physical body is gone, the love, memories and lessons learned will always be with you. You realize that you have become a better person from knowing your pet, and that your life has forever changed, not because you lost your pet, but because your pet lived and because you were fortunate enough to have shared part of your life with your pet.

When you are heartbroken after the loss of your beloved companion, it is easy to become overwhelmed by the grief and pain of the loss instead of remembering your animal companion's legacy of love. There is one simple question you can ask yourself that can help you shift your focus from the hopelessness and sorrow to the unconditional and eternal love that you share with your companion. The question is:

What if it were you?

Try for a moment to imagine that you were the one who had died, and that you were looking in from the afterlife, from the beyond, at the beloved people or animals you had to leave behind. How would you want to see them? How would you want their life to be after you have gone? Would you prefer to see loved ones in one of these states?

- Stuck in grief and sadness, hopelessness and despair, and guilt and depression
- Only seeing the emptiness and the loss
- Unable to find happiness or meaning, or make a difference in the world?

Or, would you rather see the ones you left behind live their life in one of the following ways?

- Filled with love, gratitude, inner peace and inspiration.
- Remembering with fondness and joy the love and life you had together and the lessons they have learned.
- Using that love and those lessons learned to make a difference in the world to help someone in need as you helped each other.

When you change your perspective like this, it becomes much easier to see beyond the grief and to embrace your companion's legacy of love.

Try this:

Imagine your beloved companion looking at you from the afterlife with infinite peace and love, and allow yourself to reconnect with that peace and love.

Remember that grief often comes in waves, so you might want to come back and do these exercises again to help transform your grief into inner peace, love and inspiration.

Exercise

Take a moment to note down some of the ways your life has changed and you have become a better person because of your pet.

What did you learn from the love and the life you shared with your pet?

The lessons and insights you gain from this exercise will stay with you and be the fuel and the inspiration for moving forward after the loss of your beloved pet.

Healing words from Pittiput

As I was out in the garden one morning with one of my cats, I noticed that the sun was just hitting a garden chair where Pittiput used to sit sometimes. Pittiput is my orange cat who died in June 2010, and he occasionally comes in spirit to say hello or to give advice. I received an image of him in spirit sitting on the chair in the sun, so I decided to ask him what advice he had for people whose pets had died. Here is some of what he said:

"When you have lost your pet, you tend to stay in the darkness, seeing only the grief and the separation, but that only keeps you in pain. It keeps you in grief and prevents you from connecting with your deceased animal companion, who is just waiting on the other side for you to open up to him, to receive his message, his message of love. Instead, stay in the sun, stay in the light—the inner and the outer light. Let that light enfold you, bathe in it, and you will see that the pet you have lost will come to you with a message of love, and that there is no separation. Love is not just about the physical; love is way more than that; it's beyond life and death."

I hope these words will comfort and inspire you in the midst of your grieving.

Chapter 13:
A Cat's View on Death & Tips for Living after Pet Loss

"When you arise in the morning think of what a privilege it is to be alive, to think, to enjoy, to love ..." ~ Marcus Aurelius

Have you ever wished you could hear directly from your deceased pet about how they experienced their moment of death and after? I would like to share a message I received from my beloved cat Kia a few days after she died. In this message, she describes briefly and beautifully how she experienced her own passing. She then continues with some sage advice on how to live our lives. May Kia's words help you heal after the loss of your animal companion and give you inspiration for living after your loss.

Marianne:

"Kia, my beautiful one. Can you tell me how you are doing? And can you tell me how the moment of death was for you?"

[My heart opens, and from the vast heart space a "world" pours out, a beautiful landscape with clear fresh air and the smell of flowers, and Kia sitting before me, facing me.]

Kia:

"Since I'm in your heart, I'm doing fine. It is the best place for me to be right now.

At the time of death, when the moment of fear and darkness passes, a new world appears—a world of light and love. There is a feeling of strength, and a freedom and lightness of being, and everything seems so easy. I wonder why we had all that fear.

Learn to live in the physical world without fear, so you can appreciate it while you still have your physical body and senses. My spiritual connection with you is as strong as ever, but I miss the physical contact: you touching me, holding me, or just being close to you.

Don't waste the gifts you have been given by the universe. Walk the Earth with soft steps, touching everyone you meet with your love. Love is the best remedy for fear."

Marianne:
"Thank you, Kia."

Action steps

1. Which one of Kia's messages above resonates most with you and your current situation?
2. In her message, Kia says, "Don't waste the gifts you have been given by the universe." Which steps can you take today to use your gifts? Do you know what your gifts are? If not, maybe this next period can be a journey of discovery for you.

Finding and expressing your unique gifts and sharing them with the world is a wonderful way to honor your pet's legacy.

Chapter 14:
Getting a New Pet after Pet Loss

"Perhaps they are not stars in the sky, but rather openings where our loved ones shine down to let us know they are happy." ~ Inuit saying

Although some elect to take on a new pet immediately, it is generally wiser to wait a while.

You need time to grieve and time to reflect on the life you shared with your now deceased pet—time to reflect on the special moments you had together, and time to say your goodbyes—for both your sake and for the sake of your pet.

It would also not be fair to the new pet if you were still grieving and not able to be there fully. Integrating a new pet into the household takes time, effort and your presence.

That being said, life sometimes has plans of its own and sends a new pet your way shortly after you have lost one. For instance, if a starving, homeless cat suddenly shows up on your doorstep, you will probably feel the need to take care of him or her, and you might even feel certain that it was no coincidence and you were meant to be together. Or perhaps you suddenly get a call from someone who has a puppy who desperately needs a home.

My main suggestion would be to not actively go out searching for a new pet right away and take the time you need to grieve, but to stay open and evaluate the situation if a new pet comes your way. You might even feel that it is your deceased pet sending you a companion.

The arrival of Starlight

© Marianne Soucy – www.HealingPetLoss.com

There are times when the question of whether or not to take on a new pet almost becomes irrelevant, because the universe sends a new pet your way. That is what happened a couple of months after our beloved Kia died. Suddenly, we saw a white kitten with black markings outside. As it turns out, he was wild, terrified and hungry. He must have been separated from his mother in the most terrible way, but somehow he found his way into our garden, or was guided there.

He was so small that he was still unsure on his feet, but despite his unstable walk, he managed to avoid our other cats, the neighbor's cat, and our attempts to catch him for close to a week. We put food out for him, and he managed to come out of hiding long enough to eat and drink. We could see that he was determined to stay here, and determined to survive.

Then one day, my husband finally managed to get hold of him. The kitten was so wild and afraid that he was fighting for his life, and my husband just barely made it inside with him, and not before being scratched and bitten.

We gave him his own small room and for several days, he was completely silent and so afraid that he was actually hiding behind the radiator. He was small enough that he could actually fit there; only his tiny feet, which could be seen below the radiator, revealed his hiding place. I went in several times a day to give him fresh food and water, and to spend time with him. I went about it very slowly and quietly, and did not try to approach him.

Fortunately, he was using the litter box, but he did not eat much, and he was terrified of us. We began to get concerned that he was so wild that we would never earn his trust. I decided to do a shamanic journey to communicate with the new kitten. Here is an excerpt of that journey:

As I start the journey, I find myself in a meadow on a sunny summer day. I see the white kitten come running toward me; he is almost disappearing in the tall grass. He is happy, bouncing around among the flowers, exploring the new world. He comes over to me and looks up at me, not with the look of terror and fear I have seen so far, but with a look of pure joy. "Thank you," he says, "for bringing me here." "Actually, I didn't bring you here. I just asked to connect with you"."

"Yes, but you connected with me from a place of love and light, thus inviting me here. Remember that. Bring that same love and light, and it will be much easier for me to let go of my fear and begin to trust. As you can see, my spirit is already in the light with you, so we are well on our way. Please don't give up on me. Give me time, and I will be a good kitty for you. I was ripped from safety too suddenly and too soon, and was forced to face the terrors and challenges of the big world all alone and totally unprepared. I was so lucky to discover your garden. Imagine my joy as I saw food there for the first time in days. I survived by hiding, keeping still and fighting to the death when

cornered. I did that with L when he picked me up—and I am sorry. I did not know he was not trying to kill me. Keep bringing the love and light to me when you visit me, and I will enter and heal in that love and light. Give me time, love, food and protection so I know it's safe to trust."

"Thank you so much, my beautiful one. I so appreciate you communicating with me. I have noted and will re-read every word you have said. And, by the way, thank you so much for being such a good kitty and using the litter box every time. We are impressed. Please try to eat some food and drink some water. Love you.

"Love you too," he says.

As for his name, Starlight, it was Starlight himself who let me know that he would like to be so called. He is mostly white, but has black markings and a black tail with a distinctive white tip. The white tip makes you think of a star, and it is as if Starlight is carrying his own star around with him, lighting his way, so to speak.

Soon after, he began to eat well and very slowly began to trust us more. I remember the first time he approached me: one day I was in his room with him, lying on the floor, and he came over, jumped up on me and lay there for a while, kneading on the old sweater I was wearing. It calmed him down and helped us bond—and as I write this, a little less than one year later, he sometimes still loves to lie on me and knead on that same old sweater (I keep the sweater handy).

Through all the challenges there has been one sentence he said that is forever etched into our hearts and minds: "Please don't give up on me!" He still has a lot to learn, but he has turned into a playful and loving kitty, and we love him very much.

Chapter 15:
What to Do If Your Other Pets Are Grieving the Loss of Their Animal Friend

"Grief is like the ocean; it comes on waves ebbing and flowing. Sometimes the water is calm, and sometimes it is overwhelming. All we can do is learn to swim."

~ Vicki Harrison

When you suffer the loss of a pet, it is often not just you who are grieving and having a hard time coping. If you have other pets in your household, and they have been close friends with the pet who has just died, they might be grieving too.

The signs that your pets are grieving can vary, but you will probably have noticed a change in their behavior. The grieving pets might get restless, anxious, depressed, lose their appetite, crave more attention, wander off searching for their dead animal companion, etc.

Grieving is a normal process that both humans and animals go through. Pets who have lost a friend will often get through the grieving period by themselves, but at other times, they seem to be stuck in the grieving and cannot move forward by themselves. In that case they your need help.

What you can do to help your grieving pet

If you have just lost a pet, and a surviving pet is not eating, depressed, lethargic, restless, or behaving in other ways that are out of the ordinary, there are a couple of things you can do yourself:

- Keep the grieving pet's routines as close to normal as possible.
- Have your pet checked by a vet to rule out medical issues.
- Realize that your pet is grieving just as you are—allow him or her to grieve, but be there and give extra care and attention.
- Take care of yourself and get help if needed. This will make it easier for you to be there for your grieving pet.

One thing to be aware of is that your pet can also be affected by your mood. Animals are usually very sensitive beings, so the remaining pet may not only be grieving for the loss of their animal friend but may also be deeply affected by your state of grief. This is why taking care of yourself is an important part of helping your grieving pet. For example, you could go for walks in nature or do yoga, meditation, tai chi, qi gong, etc. (see also, Chapter 9 about taking care of yourself). These are all well-known ways of becoming centered and achieving a state of inner peace.

In addition, holding a pet memorial ceremony for your deceased pet can be very helpful. You might already have had one, but if you feel you are still having a hard time coming to terms with the death of your pet, holding a ceremony where you say goodbye can help. During the ceremony you can, for example, say goodbye to your deceased pet, let them know you will be taking care of their friend left behind, and that it is okay for them to move forward on their own journey in the afterlife.

Chapter 16:
Coping with Holidays and
Anniversaries after Pet Loss

"The wound is the place where the Light enters you." ~ Rumi

Holidays and anniversaries can bring up strong feelings of grief, even a long time after the event. In this chapter, I will share a few tips for coping. Some of these tips can also be found in other chapters in this book, but they are collected here specifically to help you cope with grief during holidays and anniversaries.

Expect some feelings of sorrow or sadness

You have lost someone who was a very important part of your life, a loving friend and companion, so it is normal to grieve, even during holidays such as Christmas when you are "supposed" to be cheerful. If a holiday or an anniversary of your pet's death or birth is coming up, you may expect to experience some feelings of sorrow or sadness.

Take care of yourself

Allow yourself to grieve and take time to be alone. Seeking out the company of supportive friends or family can also be helpful. During official or traditional holidays, instead of feeling obliged to follow your usual routines and traditions, realize that it is not an ordinary holiday season if your pet is no longer with you. Look inside yourself and feel intuitively what you need to do in order to acknowledge and support yourself at this time. Some tips for taking care of yourself (see also chapter 9):

- Get enough rest and relaxation.
- Get exercise and fresh air.
- Eat healthy meals.
- Do a daily meditation to handle the feelings of grief and sorrow.

Celebrate your pet

Holidays and anniversaries do not need to be all about feeling the grief and sadness of the loss of your pet. They also present a perfect opportunity for you to celebrate the love you shared, the joy your pet brought into your life, and the lessons you learned from them. Include your pet when you plan your holiday celebrations. If a holiday is coming up shortly after you have lost a pet, you could even give the celebrations a focus on honoring and celebrating your pet. For anniversaries you could, for example, create a memorial ceremony for your pet; plant a flower, bush or tree in your pet's honor; or revisit some of the places where you used to spend time with your pet.

Tips and action steps

Below are a few suggestions for ways to cope with the loss of your pet during holidays, and several of the suggestions can be used for anniversaries.

- Take a look at the things you usually do during holidays—can any of those things or traditions be changed, modified or eliminated?
- Begin your holiday dinner with a quiet moment in honor of your pet.

- When your family gathers together, take some time to share fond memories you all have of your pet.
- Play songs that remind you of your pet.
- Create special rituals or celebrations that honor your pet:
- Light a candle in your pet's honor.
- If you celebrate Christmas, hang up a special Christmas stocking for your pet and find some meaningful items to place inside, for example, a special toy your pet liked, a photo, a little poem or letter you have written to your pet—whatever feels right. Do this as a conscious process that is light and joyful, and each time you see the stocking you will feel joy and connection with your pet. You may feel inspired at times to look at the items in the stocking and perhaps read aloud the poem or letter that you have placed there.
- Create an altar with special things that remind you of your pet, where you can sit and reflect on the life and love you shared.
- Reach out for support.
- Help an animal in need.

Use your imagination and be creative when celebrating and honoring your pet during holidays and anniversaries. There is no right or wrong way to do this. Do what feels right to you.

Chapter 17:
Children and Pet Loss - A True Story & 5 Tips to Help Your Children Grieve When They Lose a Pet

"We'll be friends forever, won't we, Pooh?' asked Piglet.
Even longer,' Pooh answered."

~ A.A. Milne, Winnie the Pooh

This chapter is based on my own experience with pet loss as a child. It is not meant to cover everything there is to know about children and pet loss, but it will show you:

- The strength of the bond that can exist between a child and his or her pet.
- The deep impact and long-lasting effects that the loss of a pet can have on a child.
- What can happen when the adults do not acknowledge pet loss, and do not know how to deal with loss themselves or do not know how to help their child.
- The importance of you as an adult being able to cope with your own feelings of grief and loss.
- Five tips for helping your child cope with the loss a pet.

Let us begin with the true story of the summer when my best friend was a little black kitten.

The little black cat—the summer I will never forget

© Marianne Soucy - www.HealingPetLoss.com

The following took place during one summer when I was just about ten years old. What happened has had such a deep impact on me and my life that I finally decided to share it so that others might learn how deep a friendship can be between a little girl and a cat, and how important it is to educate adults about compassion—to be able to see past our own fears and limitations, and respect and reach out to animals who need our help.

I grew up in a big city in an apartment building with ten apartments, two storefronts and—best of all—a magical back garden. It was a little paradise with roses, lilacs, a big birch tree and a little old pear tree bearing the best pears I have ever tasted. My grandmother lived there too, and she was the owner of the building.

One summer day, we had a visitor to the garden: a little black kitten. I quickly formed a friendship with the little cat. He was so full of joy and unconditional love. Every day, when I came home from school, he would be waiting, and he would come to me when I called. Unfortunately, my grandmother did not like cats, so I was not allowed to feed him, and my parents wanted to avoid problems with my grandmother, so they did not argue with her decision. It hurt me so much not to be able to feed the hungry little cat, but fortunately some other people in the building secretly put food out for him.

The friendship and connection with a cat—or any animal, for that matter—can sometimes be deeper than with a human, because the animal doesn't judge you, but loves you as you are, and the connection is so true and pure. I remember the little cat running around happily in the rose bed among the blooming roses. He even allowed me to pick him up and hold him in my arms.

One day in particular stands out. It was a warm, sunny day, and I was down in the garden with the little cat. I had found a spot that was hidden from all the windows in the buildings surrounding us. I was lying on my stomach, resting in the sun, and the little black cat decided to lie on my back. He lay there for a long time, curled up, sleeping, and I did not dare move. But that feeling of closeness and deep peace as the cat was lying on my back was amazing and impossible to describe, and I will never forget it. He had not been in my life for long, but he was my closest friend.

Then suddenly, one day when I came home from school, he was gone! Just like that. It turned out that the adults had taken him away. Not only was that a totally horrible and unnecessary thing to do, especially without asking for my opinion, but I had not even had a chance to say goodbye to him. I was in shock, and I can still feel it now when I think of it.

The story they gave me was that one of the storekeepers in the building knew a farmer, and that the cat was now on that farm. I never really believed that story, but I was too afraid of what I might hear if I dug deeper.

The cat—or rather, kitten—was so beautiful, loving, trusting and playful, and did not bother anyone. I could not understand—and still cannot to this day—how people could do a thing like that. It is scary that an irrational fear of and prejudice against cats can lead someone to do such a thing—to separate two best friends. He could have had a wonderful life with us. However, I have reminded myself many times that neither my grandmother nor my parents knew any better.

This has obviously affected me deeply, and I still sometimes catch myself being upset with the people who took my friend away. Holding grudges does not get us anywhere, so I decided to make up for it in any way I could from then on. My husband and I have never actively looked for a cat, but somehow we have several times stumbled upon cats in desperate need of help. And guess what? The first one to come to us for help was a black cat! That cat was Kia, and she was a truly wonderful cat and a special friend of mine. We were fortunate to share twelve wonderful years with her before she passed in 2012.

This story is in loving memory of that first little black kitten that has a special place in my heart.

5 tips to help your child cope with pet loss

Tip #1: Acknowledge the child's grief

Acknowledge that the child is grieving, and do not underestimate the depth of the grief a child can experience. The human–animal bond can be very strong, and that applies to both adults and children. The animal might have been the child's best friend; the only one they felt loved them unconditionally.

It is important to let the child say goodbye to the pet, if possible. Do not simply remove it. Never say things like, for example, "it was just a guinea pig; we can get another one." The type or size of the animal is not relevant here—only the strength of the bond there was between the pet and the child.

How you handle grief teaches the child how to handle it—it is ok to show sadness, both of you. Do not forget to make decisions about the pet with the child and with respect for the child and his or her closeness to the pet. Do not make decisions based solely on your own feelings or irrational fear.

Tip #2: Be honest and clear in what you say

Avoid saying things like, "he has gone to sleep" or other things that might be misunderstood by the child. Be sure to let the child know that the pet is not coming back. How you describe death to your child will depend on the child's age.

Do not try to "protect" or shield the child by withholding information, lying or excluding the child. Of course, you must evaluate what and how much you say and involve the child, and that can be very individual depending on the child's age and emotional attachment to the pet, and the circumstances surrounding the pet's death.

Based on my personal experience, it is not a good idea to go behind a child's back and, for instance, take away or euthanize a pet and then follow up by lying to the child about what happened. "He is living on a farm and is happy now" does not work and can hurt the child for life. Remember that the animal may have been the child's best friend, so it is essential that they are involved in what happens.

Tip #3: Create a pet memorial ceremony

Involve the child in the burial and in creating a pet memorial ceremony. How does the child wish to say goodbye to the pet? A pet memorial ceremony could include the following:

- lighting a candle next to a photo of the pet, and maybe having the pet's collar or favorite toys nearby;

- writing and reading a poem or letter you or the child (or both) have written to or about the pet;
- planting a tree or flower in the garden, or in a pot if you don't have a garden;
- burying your pet's body in a special place in the garden (if you don't have a garden, find a special place, or you could also investigate if there is a pet cemetery near you);
- scattering the pet's ashes in a place that was special to the pet and you;
- taking a walk you used to do with your pet, or spending time in some of your pet's favorite places, and either spending time there silently contemplating your pet or sharing fond memories;
- some other ways of remembering the pet:
- keep a special journal dedicated to the pet where the child writes stories about, or sends letters to the pet.
- make drawings of the pet;
- make a scrapbook or photo collage

See also Chapter 6, How to create your own pet memorial ceremony.

Tip #4: Listen to your child—and be prepared to answer questions

Let your child speak about the pet—and listen. Let your child express feelings and thoughts about loss and death. Be prepared to answer questions that the child has about death. If the child asks questions about death you do not know the answers to, it is okay to say that you do not know.

As for where the pet has gone, try to listen first, to what the child has to say. For example, let the child imagine where the pet is now. When the child can imagine their pet being happy, you have both taken a big step toward healing.

Share memories—and perhaps tears. Help your child remember all the good times with their pet.

Tip #5: Avoid getting a new pet right away

If the child had a close relationship with the pet, just getting a replacement pet is, in most cases, not a good idea. The pet was more than a pet to the child—it was perhaps their closest friend, a family member, like a sibling. The child needs time to grieve. Wait before taking on a new pet until the child can speak without pain about the pet they have lost and express interest in getting a new pet.

A close friend cannot be replaced. Wait until the time is right and you are all ready to receive a new pet into the family. When the child—or the family as a whole—is ready for a new pet is very individual, so you will have to evaluate the situation when it arises.

Dealing with your own grief in order to help your child

Pets nowadays are often members of the family, and the bond between the human members and the pet can be very strong. If you have had a close and loving relationship with the pet who has just died, you will also be grieving deeply and need to find ways of coping with your own grief.

When you have children who are also grieving the loss of the beloved pet, it can be helpful to remember that you as an adult are a role model for the child. How you cope with your own feelings about death, and your loss and grief will determine how well you are able to support and guide your child.

You cannot help the child efficiently deal with the loss if you are not able to cope with loss yourself. Therefore, it is necessary that you to deal with your own grief so that you can be there for and guide your child through his or her grief. Grief and loss is going to be part of the child's life sooner or later, so it is important that you allow the child to grieve, and that you support them through the period after the loss.

Several of the tips can also help you in your own grieving process:

- keep a journal
- create or take part in a pet memorial ceremony
- allow yourself to grieve the loss of your beloved animal companion

Chapter 18:
Using Animal and Spirit Wisdom to Cope with a Missing Pet

"We sit together quietly in peace for a while here in my heart – one place I know he is safe. It is a sanctuary and a healing place for him and a wonderful place for us to connect." ~ Marianne Soucy

When a beloved pet goes missing, the uncertainty and fear of what may have happened can be devastating. Not only can your mind come up with all kinds of horrible scenarios for what could have happened to your animal companion, but it is also possible that feelings of guilt and self-blame will torment you.

There are many practical steps you can take to search for and announce locally and online that your pet is missing—a simple Internet search will bring up many helpful websites. Even though you have taken all the steps you can, dealing with the emotions evoked by the loss of your animal friend is very difficult. The uncertainty is especially hard to handle, as it can keep you in long-term emotional turmoil, switching from feelings of hope one minute to despair and grief the next.

Rumi—a loving pet lost in a tragic accident

I have also experienced missing a beloved pet who has disappeared. One day my black-and-white Manx cat, Rumi, did not come home from his nightly rounds. My husband and I experienced several days of emotional torment before we got a call from a kind woman after she saw one of our flyers. She told us that she recognized Rumi's photo from the flyer and that she had seen our precious Rumi lying dead in the street, apparently the victim of a hit-and-run driver. Even though we had suspected and tried to prepare for the possibility that he was dead, it was still heartbreaking to get confirmation that Rumi was gone and that we would never see him again.

However, knowing what happened is not all bad, even when it is discovered that your beloved pet has died. The pain of the loss is still overwhelming, but knowing that their life has ended brings a degree of closure, and therefore peace. The not knowing, I find, is very hard and makes it nearly impossible to get closure or relief. The constant wondering what happened and hoping for a beloved pet's return can be debilitating.

Receiving confirmation that Rumi was dead enabled us to say goodbye to him, make a memorial ceremony for him and express our gratitude for the love and joy he brought into our lives. He sent me a message from beyond, "Remember the love." And I do. He even sent a special sign from beyond to my husband and me. (See "Rumi and the cherry blossoms" in Chapter 7 about synchronicities.)

When Freedom was missing for five days

We have another cat who joined us a while after Rumi had died. He is a tuxedo cat whose name, Freedom, is apt—he is a free spirit who loves his freedom and sometimes goes traveling. He is a lone wolf (he even has a wolf as his spirit helper). It takes a long time to get to know Freedom, but it has been worth every effort ten times over. Freedom is very affectionate and extremely sensitive. He sometimes goes exploring for a day or so, but when he was missing for five days, we were afraid we had lost him.

Every time I went to check if he had snuck in the cat door without us noticing and I found his chair empty, my heart sank.

Kia's helpful advice

One thing that really helped us through those five days was some advice I got from Kia, my beloved angel cat who died in July 2012 and who brings me wisdom and comfort from the afterlife. Her words helped me make the mindset shift needed to best be there for the absent Freedom. Here is an excerpt from what Kia said:

Never let the fear and dark thoughts take over. Whether Freedom is alive or dead, he needs your loving thoughts. Let the light in your heart shine with the brightest light you can, so he can find his way home—in spirit or his physical body. Hold the image of him in your light and love—it means more than you think.

~ Kia

May Kia's words help your heart shine with the brightest light possible for your beloved pet who is missing.

PS: On the evening of the fifth day, we suddenly heard the cat door, and when we went out to check, there was Freedom. We had almost given up on ever seeing him again, so it was such a gift to get him back again. He had lost some weight and had been in a fight, but was otherwise okay. Sometimes miracles do happen, and to us Freedom's return after he had been missing for five days was an absolute miracle.

Connecting with a missing pet

When a beloved pet is missing, besides desperately wanting our companion back, we have an even deeper desire (even if we do not realize it) to connect with them wherever they are, whether in this life or beyond. There are many ways you can connect with your pet in spirit and thus regain some peace of mind.

When my beloved cat Freedom went missing for five days, the only place I could connect with him was in my heart. At the time, I did not know whether he was dead or alive. This is an excerpt from my connection with Freedom in my heart.

When I think of Freedom and try to connect with him, I can only do so in my heart. I experience my heart space as a garden. It looks like my real-life garden. I go to the chair that Freedom often lies on and I put a towel on the chair to make it comfortable for him. The chair is placed in a protected place in front of some bushes in the sun. And then—just as he usually does in "real life", Freedom comes running and jumps up on the chair. He is happy.

I bend down, my face close to his, and tell him how much I love him. He rests his head against mine; so much gentle love.

We sit together quietly in peace for a while here in my heart— one place I know he is safe. It is a sanctuary and a healing place for him and a wonderful place for us to connect.

Experiencing that connection with Freedom in my heart allowed me to let go of the worry and fear I had and to regain some peace of mind. I knew that whether he was alive or not, I now had a way and a place to connect with him.

A dog's message of peace

One of the keys to both coping with and connecting with a missing pet is achieving a state of peace and calm. I have had pets go missing myself, so I know that is easier said than done. However, I have found it helpful to strive to achieve a balance between allowing yourself to feel whatever you are feeling—fear, worry, etc.—and avoiding letting the negative and fearful thoughts take control.

I will shortly offer a few tips for achieving inner peace, but first I will share a communication I had with a missing dog. If you are currently looking for ways to cope with a missing animal companion, I hope that the dog's message to their human caretaker will inspire you:

As I connect with the dog, I first experience the situation from the dog's point of view. As the dog, I experience myself down low, coming out between some bushes. I feel as if I don't know where I am. Something or someone big approaches. I first think it's my human, but it's not. In an instant, I lose consciousness. When I awake, I see my human sitting, crying. I go to her, but she doesn't see me. I'm confused. I bark but she doesn't hear. I look around, puzzled, afraid.

A spirit guide comforts me, asking if I want to send a message, a sign. "Yes!"

"But she'll only see the sign if she calms down and pays attention," the spirit guide says. He drops a ball in front of her—she doesn't see it, but hears it. She knows the sound.

I'm now my own self again and I see the little dog jump up on the woman's lap and lick her face—she feels something and touches the place on her cheek where the dog licked her.

"Tell her I love her very much," the dog says to me. "I'm very sad to be away from her, but she would help me if she were happy. Tell her to think of all the good times we had; tell her to imagine me in my favorite spot, us together, in love and peace. That will help me more than anything else will. She has so much love to give—don't waste it. Use it to share with and help someone who needs her love. We will meet again. Until then, tell her we can reconnect in dreams and meditations. I will meet her in places and times of peace. Return to the peace—it is easier for me to access her there. I must move on but will be available to her, as we are forever connected by the love we shared. Surrender to love (not fear or pain)."

I ask the dog, "Are you okay now?" And the dog answers, "Yes, I'm at peace now."

What especially strikes me in this dog's message is how it is easier for the dog to access or connect with their human when the human is at peace. While it may certainly be difficult to achieve a state of calm and peace when a beloved animal companion is missing, it is essentially what is needed to reconnect.

Suggestions for gaining inner peace

Some helpful suggestions for achieving a state of inner peace and calm:

- Spend time in nature.
- Do yoga, tai chi or qi gong.
- Meditate.
- Listen to soothing music.
- Do garden work.

Ask yourself, "How can I reach a state of inner peace and calm?" Then take steps to integrate that into your daily life.

Exercise for connecting with a missing pet

The technique I used to connect with Freedom is quite simple, and if you wish to connect with your missing animal companion, you can try it too.

1. Use a meditation or some relaxing music to become calm and focused.
2. Set the intention to connect with your missing pet.
3. Focus on your heart center in the middle of your chest. Go into that heart space and see it filled with light. Notice what your heart space looks and feels like; maybe you experience a sacred garden, a landscape, or perhaps a healing light.

You can either use the image that comes up or, if no particular image comes up, imagine your pet's favorite place. Imagine being in a place your pet loves, where you usually connect with your pet in real life. Feel yourself in that space, peacefully waiting. Try not to feel desperate or too eager—just allow yourself to rest in peaceful confidence, sending out a loving thought to your pet, "I'm here". Imagine your pet approaching and greeting you lovingly. Spend some time feeling the togetherness, and if it feels right, ask your pet a question and see if an answer comes to you.

This exercise does not need to be complicated or elaborate— even just making a connection, or getting a feeling or a glimpse of your pet can have a deep impact.

Even if you did not feel you made a connection with your pet, do not worry; just sending out your loving intention from a place of peace can make a very big difference both for you and for your pet.

Moving forward when your pet is missing

The loss of a beloved pet is a heartbreaking experience that can turn your whole world upside down. If you are in a situation where your pet has gone missing, it can be very hard to cope, let alone move forward.

Moving forward will be different for you, depending on which of these three scenarios is relevant to you:

1. Your missing pet is alive and returns to you.
2. Your missing pet turns out to be dead.
3. You do not receive confirmation of whether your pet is dead or alive, and you must live with the uncertainty.

Moving forward when your missing pet returns to you alive

If you are lucky enough to be reunited with your beloved pet after they have been missing, you will feel that you have experienced a miracle, and that you have been given a second chance.

If you feel like I did when my cat Freedom came home after having been missing for five days, you will want to make the most of the time you have left with your pet. The reality and pain that someday your pet will not be there with you anymore has hit you hard. When you have been given the gift of more time with your precious companion, my suggestions for you are twofold:

A) Practice being present with your pet

How often in our lives are we busy doing something or worrying about something, and not 100 percent present when spending time with our pet. They want to play or spend time with us, but we do not have the time or are only partly there with them. When you are reunited with your pet after they have been missing, you have a great opportunity to practice present-moment awareness. That presence and calm you achieve will carry over into the rest of your life. Meditation is a useful tool for learning and practicing present-moment awareness.

B) Practice gratitude

Besides the sheer joy of seeing your animal companion again after they have been missing, a dominant feeling is gratitude. You have truly been given a gift, and now is a good time to begin to consciously practicing gratitude.

We may often take our loved ones for granted and fail to express our gratitude and love by, for instance, appreciating the small things that sometimes mean so much. Practicing gratitude means becoming conscious about your blessings, and noticing and giving thanks for the little things in your life, but also seeing and appreciating the big picture. For example, look at what lessons your pet is here to teach you.

When you find out that your missing pet has died

Learning that your beloved animal companion has died after having been missing is devastating. Not only has your pet been removed suddenly and unexpectedly from your life, but you also did not have a chance to say goodbye or be there for them when they died. On top of that, overwhelming feelings of guilt are likely to surface, because you may blame yourself for failing to protect or save your trusted friend. I am familiar with all those feelings, because that's how I felt when my beloved cat Rumi died tragically and suddenly. If you find out that your animal companion has died, the exercises, techniques, inspiration and insights you will find throughout this book can be helpful to you. I have used them myself to cope with the death of a beloved pet.

When you have to live with the uncertainty

Sometimes surrendering means giving up trying to understand and becoming comfortable with not knowing. ~ Eckhart Tolle

Having to live with the uncertainty of your pet's fate is very challenging, because it means living with the constant hope that your pet might be alive and well, while at the same time fearing they are deceased or suffering. It can be almost impossible to move forward; because we do not want to give up hope if there is even the slightest chance our trusted friend might be alive.

At some point, we need to surrender, which means giving up trying to understand and becoming comfortable with not knowing, as Eckhart Tolle says in the quote above. It does not mean giving up all hope of seeing your pet again; it simply means learning to live with the uncertainty.

One exercise that can be helpful is that where you connect with your missing pet, as mentioned in the previous section. This exercise can be done whether your pet is alive or deceased.

Animal wisdom—awakening and restoring your sense of wonder

Wonder is as necessary to life as the very air we breathe and the food we eat. ~ Ted Andrews

We can also turn to the wisdom of animals to help us cope and move forward when our beloved pet is missing. I would like to share a couple of excerpts from my communications with an owl and a unicorn that took place when my cat Freedom was missing for five days. May their wise words give you comfort and insight.

The owl hoots and speaks: "What is hidden shall be revealed. See with your mind's eye, and with your heart. If you use your normal senses, you are missing out on much. Step beyond your limiting beliefs and realize there are no limits, no boundaries, no separateness. You cannot be separated from what has been yours—and part of you—all along. Wherever Freedom is, he is not separate from you. Connect with him in love, in your heart, and realize that you are one."

I just manage to think, "Is Freedom okay?" as a magnificent unicorn shows up, a soft light surrounding him.

The unicorn says, "Blessings to you all for coming, for caring and for stepping beyond your doubts to embrace what cannot be seen. When you embrace the magic in your heart, you will enable it to manifest the magic in ordinary life. Losses—and potential losses—are great healing and learning experiences. In this case, you grieve deeply the loss of Freedom, even though you truly don't know yet if he is dead or alive. Your mind tells you he is probably dead, so you grieve. You are not grieving an actual loss, but an imagined loss. Ultimately, all losses are imagined, for if you learn how to connect in spirit, in love—

beyond the physical—then you realize that the physical is illusory, and that love and spirit are eternal. Feel the love and light when you connect with Freedom in your heart—that is the truth. That is the legacy you carry with you, sharing it with others and showing them to access the love and light in their own heart. Call on me for healing and insight."

In answer to my question about Freedom's well-being and whereabouts, the unicorn answers: "Look again in your heart. For now, keep returning to your heart."

As you can see from above, the animals we can connect with and learn from are not just ordinary, "real-life" animals, but also magical creatures like the unicorn. If you are a skeptic, that is okay, but try to keep an open mind—or perhaps, especially, an open heart. First, try to focus on the message of the unicorn instead of thinking too much about whether it is real or not. Second, before you dismiss the unicorn, its existence and teachings, please read this very special poem about a man in search of a unicorn. It is called "Ragged John," and it moves me deeply each time I read it. You can find the poem via an Internet search. You can also read the poem in Ted Andrew's book, Treasures of the Unicorn, which I can highly recommend. At the beginning of the book, Ted Andrews describes his own encounter with a unicorn, which he had as a boy.

On the practical side

Doing the exercise to connect with your pet using the wisdom of animals to cope and move forward when your pet is missing can be very helpful in your healing process. However, the practical side is just as important. When your pet is missing, taking the right steps to find your pet can determine whether you succeed or not. The many practical steps you can take to find your missing pet are beyond the scope of this book. A simple Internet search will lead you to many helpful websites.

Chapter 19:
Animals As Teachers
- An Introduction

"Let the light and joy in me connect you with the light and joy within yourself. It is actually quite simple. Deep gratitude combined with joy makes you shine. Your soul reveals its true essence – timeless bliss." ~ Minnie

This chapter is not meant to cover all there is to know about animals as teachers, but is simply meant to raise your awareness and point out that animals have many lessons to teach us. Here, we will focus on some of the lessons that your own pet can teach you.

From your own life with your animal companion, you will have experienced the close bond that is formed between you and your animal companion. You will have experienced the love and joy that your pet has brought into your life, as well as the challenges. It may not have occurred to you before that your pet could be your teacher. If you look more closely, however, you will discover that your pet, besides bringing you love and joy, has many different lessons to teach and much wisdom to share.

Pets as teachers

Pets can teach us many things:

- unconditional love
- non-judgment
- being present
- joy
- playfulness
- loyalty
- forgiveness
- gratitude
- openness
- letting go
- inner peace
- contentedness

Our pets often reflect our own personal issues, and if we become aware of them, we can work through them and thus evolve as human beings. Each animal has unique qualities that you can appreciate and learn from. Let me give you an example.

Minnie's arrival

My cat Minnie is a wonderful kitty that came to us one morning in October 2011. My husband and I were getting ready to go out for the day. It was very early and still dark outside. As we passed by our garage, we heard a desperate meow and saw a cat sitting there. She was very skinny and obviously starving. As I approached her, she did not become afraid, but stayed where she was and let me pick her up. I would not normally try to pick up a cat I did not know, but I reacted intuitively and sensed that this cat was a special case. She was in very bad shape, and we were clearly her last chance for survival.

As I picked her up, I discovered that she weighed almost nothing. I carried her inside, and she did not resist at all, but instead relaxed in my arms.

Setting boundaries to create peace

Minnie felt at home right away and decided to carve out her place among the other four cats. Whenever one of the others came too close, she hissed. Despite her frequent hissing at the beginning, integration with the other cats went surprisingly well, mainly because of her unique ability to mix inner peace with fiercely standing up for herself when necessary. Actually, her ability to stand up for herself and set boundaries is an important lesson she has to teach, and an example that I believe many of us could learn from.

Beaming gratitude

One of Minnie's most amazing qualities is her almost constant display of gratitude. Ever since she found us and we rescued her that morning, her gratitude toward us has been infinite. She not only shows us gratitude, but also literally beams joy and gratitude much of the time. That is the best way I can explain it, although this quality of Minnie's has proved difficult to capture on film.

When we go to sleep at night, she comes up, lays on my chest with her face no more than a few inches away from mine, and then looks at me with half-closed eyes and purrs for a long time. When she is outside in the garden under supervision (usually with harness and leash), she pauses regularly, throws back her head and looks up at us, beaming joy and gratitude.

We feel blessed by her infinite and constant display of gratitude, and she teaches us to look at ourselves and to investigate in what areas of our lives we need to feel more appreciation and show more gratitude. It is so easy to take things, people, pets and our lives for granted. We take Minnie's lessons to heart and are grateful for being blessed with having Minnie in our lives.

There is much more to tell about Minnie, but that will have to wait until another time. For now, let us help you to take your next step in discovering and embracing your own beloved animal companion as a teacher.

Your next step

Looking at what lessons your pet has for you is a powerful exercise that you can use both when your pet is alive and after your pet is gone. After the loss of your beloved animal companion, diving into the subject of what lessons you have learned—and are still learning—from your pet, can be very rewarding and healing. Embracing those lessons can help you move more easily through your grief after the loss and enable you to reach a place of peace, gratitude and inspiration.

What lessons have you learned from your pet?

Chapter 20:
A Real-Life Example of Connecting with a Pet in the Afterlife

".. I am your little light now and forever. Be happy and share my light where you can. That's the best way you can honor me." ~ an Angel Dog

A woman approached me, devastated by the loss of her beloved dog that had been part of her life for the past 12 years. A big family vacation had been planned for over a year and the day before they were to leave, their dog suddenly became ill. The vet diagnosed him with congestive heart failure and gave the dog an injection and some medication for the woman to give to her dog, telling them to return in two weeks' time. After careful consideration, they decided to go on the vacation and leave the dog home with someone who would watch and care for him while they were gone. At the time they left, the dog's health was about the same, not better but not worse. Unfortunately, while they were gone, the dog quickly got worse and died the day before they arrived home. The woman was heartbroken with guilt for not staying home and being there when her dog died and asked how she could possibly forgive herself and move on after that.

As I usually do, I tuned in to my spirit helpers to access their vast well of wisdom and compassion. What came out of it was the following magical journey, and the dog returned with a most beautiful message that I share here so that others who find themselves in a similar situation may receive comfort and healing in the midst of their own grief.

Here is what happened:

I start by becoming present in my body. That is always the first step. Being here now, not wanting or trying to be any place else. Then I find myself on a beach, standing at the edge of the sea with the waves gently lapping and touching my feet. I feel the air, fresh sea air, on my body, and breathe it in. I take a deep breath and exhale stress, confusion, and inhale focus, strength, light - doing it until I radiate light.

One of my spirit guides comes out from the shade between some trees with a woman. I say her name. She looks up and nods. She is sad.

I greet her warmly. She says, "How do I let go of guilt? I should have been there. He died without me." Her tears are rolling down her cheeks.

My spirit guide takes her hand. "Look", he says and points out over the sea. The sun is shining on the water, shimmering, like little diamonds. Suddenly out of the light appears a dog, radiating the brightest and most beautiful light as he sits before her. She squints and looks, and then she calls out the dog's name in amazement.

The dog makes a little "Woof" and says, "I'm glad I finally got to talk with you. I am here to bring you blessings and light. I was a light in your life when I was alive. Let me continue to be a light on your path through life now that I have passed. It is only my physical body that's gone, remember that. My spirit is strong and radiating the light and love that I have always been a channel for. It is my ability to love unconditionally that allows me to embody and pass on such light and love. Don't dwell on the events leading up to my death. You did the best you could with the knowledge you had, and you need to forgive yourself. Let the unconditional love you have for me also include yourself. When you allow yourself to live and act from a place of unconditional love, you have fulfilled your life's purpose. I am your little light now and forever. Be happy and share my light where you can. That's the best way you can honor me."

She bends down and embraces the dog, and the dog's light surround them both, and as she gets up, she's standing more straight, and the darkness she had been carrying is now gone and replaced with light and joy.

She thanks the dog and waves joyfully to him as he returns to the light from which he came." I will always remember this meeting", she says. "How could I have forgotten he's my little light? Nothing can ever take that away. Now I know he's by my side lighting my way." She looks with gratitude out over the sea at the light dancing on the water.

"Thank you", she says to us. Then we say goodbye and she walks off.

I thank my spirit guides for their help.

I hope the dog's beautiful message will bring peace and healing to you, and comfort you in your time of grief after losing your beloved animal companion.

Chapter 21:
Additional Resources

In this chapter, you will find new helpful resources, as well as a listing of some of the resources mentioned throughout the book.

How to use Pinterest to heal after pet loss

When we are grieving the loss of a pet, we can express our feelings, and share our stories and love for them in many ways. Some of the known ways are writing, drawing and painting.

A traditional and time-honored way of commemorating, honoring and celebrating our deceased pet is to create a collage of photos and memorabilia so we feel a connection with our pet by looking at it. It has recently become very easy to create a digital collage online and share our sentiments with others. We now have access to a new and exciting way of sharing pictures and stories about our pet with other people, and that is Pinterest.

Pinterest is a virtual pin board which lets users organize things they like, such as images and videos, and share them with others. The images or videos you upload, or re-pin from someone else's board, are called pins, and they can be grouped into boards (as in pin board), which are sets of pins focused on a specific topic.

Examples of how to use Pinterest after the death of a pet

You can create a 'pin board' dedicated to your deceased pet and pin or share on the board:

- photos of your pet
- a photo collage you have made of your pet
- a short video of your pet
- a quote that touches you and reminds you of your pet
- photos of places, toys etc. that your pet liked

If you are uploading your own photos, it is a good idea to put a watermark or copyright notice on them, as they are likely to be re-pinned by others. Animal photos are very popular on Pinterest, and you will find many beautiful (and cute) animal photos there, which you may re-pin to your own boards. Other people can also Like and re-pin your pins. Pinterest quotes are also very popular, so you can easily find many comforting, inspiring and beautiful quote images there.

Check out and connect with Healing Pet Loss on Pinterest at www.pinterest.com/healingpetloss

Other helpful resources

On the resource page on HealingPetLoss.com you can find links to other helpful tools and resources, some of them mentioned in this book. You can for instance find links to the following:

Music for healing and peace

Songs for pet loss and grief healing

Journal for Healing Pet Loss

Gratitude Journal

Inner Peace Meditation

An Easy Exercise For Connecting With A Pet In The Afterlife

The meditation: A Sacred Meeting In A Magical Garden

The meditation: Into The Light

And, much more . . .

Resource page: http://www.HealingPetLoss.com/resources

An Invitation

I invite you to connect with Healing Pet Loss on **Facebook** for further support, inspiration, resources, and news. It is also a good place to connect with me directly and ask questions.

To visit Healing Pet Loss on Facebook, go to
http://www.facebook.com/healingpetloss

About the Author

Marianne Soucy is the author of the books, "Healing Pet Loss: Practical Steps for Coping and Comforting Messages from Animals and Spirit Guides" and "Gathering The Light – Healing, Inspiration and Empowerment through Animal Messages and Journeys Into Spirit". She is also the creator of the guided meditation, Inner Peace Meditation. Marianne is a Healing Pet Loss Guide, a Life Coach, and the founder of Healing Pet Loss and HealingPetLoss.com. Marianne has experienced pet loss several times herself, and her experience, combined with wisdom and insights from her long-term spiritual practices and ongoing research, has enabled her to develop highly effective practical techniques for healing pet loss.

I hope you have found this book helpful. If you wish to learn more, please visit my website:

http://www.healingpetloss.com

where you can find more comfort, inspiration, and information on coping and healing after the loss of a beloved animal companion.

Peace and blessings,

Marianne Soucy

The book is also available in Kindle format on Amazon.

Notes

These pages can be used for your own personal notes.

Made in the USA
Las Vegas, NV
02 April 2023

70044442R00066